The Monm‹

and the Bloody Assizes

Geoff Sawers

Two Rivers Press

2007

First published in December 1999 by
Two Rivers Press
35–39 London Street
Reading RG1 4PS

Second edition January 2007

Edited and designed by Goober Fox
Typeset in Garamond 11/12
Printed and bound by Wessex Malthouse, Taunton

9781901677492

The Prospect

History is seamless. But, if we must pick a thread and start this story somewhere, then the port of Dover in the year 1670 is as good a place and time as any. The occasion is the brokering of a secret treaty of peace and alliance between England and France. Catholic France wants to carve up the erstwhile Protestant alliance of Holland, England and Sweden; if possible, to carve up England itself. And King Charles II of England, the 'Merry Monarch', and as improvident as he is undoubtedly merry, is, to put it bluntly, broke. Handsome, witty, and indescribably lazy, this was the Charles who had inspired the poet John Wilmot to compose for him a premature epitaph which ran

> Here lies our Sovereign Lord the King
> Whose promise none relies on.
> He never said a foolish thing
> Nor ever did a wise one.

In the generally porous circles of the Restoration court, such a jibe was bound to find its way back to the king's ear; who, having as little malice in him as he had application, simply responded in kind:

> Quite so, for my words are my own, but my actions, they are my ministers'.

But at the conference of Dover, Charles does for once act for himself. Whether he does so wisely or foolishly is a matter later hotly debated, though it will be many years before the details of this treaty become public. Away from the eyes of parliament, and through the careful negotiation of his Catholic younger sister (married to the French king's oafish brother) he signs up to what is perhaps the most ignominious contract ever signed by a British monarch. In order to avoid the humiliation of going begging regularly to parliament for more money, Charles accepts a pension from Louis XIV of France. His own side of the bargain has two parts. Firstly, he agrees to renege on his former alliance with Holland and instead, with France, attack her. Secondly, and crucially for this story, he agrees to become a Catholic himself, and leave a Catholic on the throne at his death.

As easy as it was for many to be shocked at the sight of a king so casually betraying his country, it may be hard for some in more secular times to understand why this constituted a betrayal at all. To do so we need to picture England as it saw itself then; an heroic flag-bearer for the true faith of Protestantism, standing virtually alone on the edge of Europe under constant threat from the far larger (and richer) Catholic kingdoms of France and Spain. The secret treaty of Dover was possibly the most subtle of all the many Catholic plots, and very nearly succeeded in making England a vassal of France.

Charles was not, it should be stressed, agreeing to Catholicise England; he was astute enough to recognise the frailty of his position as king. His father, Charles I, leaning too far toward Catholicism and arbitrary government, had paid for the dalliance with his life. For Charles II to do the same would probably start a second civil war, one that he would have been by no means certain of winning. He knew that he had been invited back from exile to take the throne only because Oliver Cromwell's son Richard had failed to do as his father had done and hold the Government and Army together.

Charles was, in 1670, still trying to consolidate his position as king; and for this he needed an heir. He had married, in 1662, the Portuguese Princess Catherine of Bragança but, despite all the king's efforts, his placid and pious queen remained childless. After 8 years of marriage, this was causing some alarm in the kingdom of England, and to this alarm was added frustration at the seeming ease with which the king's mistresses bore him bastards. There were already seven by the time he married; at his death he acknowledged twice that number. Barbara Palmer – married off to the (at first) unsuspecting Lord Castlemaine – alone bore him five.

In the year of his marriage, the young King Charles brought over to the English court the eldest of these bastards, heir to the throne if only he had been legitimate; a strapping and lively lad of 13 named James Scott. Charles doted upon the boy, swiftly marrying him to a rich heiress, creating him a Knight of the Garter, and bestowing on him the title of Duke of Monmouth.

The new duke's mother was one Lucy Walter, a Welsh 'strumpet' whom the diarist John Evelyn had described as 'a brown [i.e. brown-haired], beautiful, bold, but insipid creature'; Aubrey wrote that she 'could deny nobody'. Certainly she could not deny the young Charles Stuart when she met him in his years of exile from the English Commonwealth. Both were 18 at the time, and within a year Lucy was pregnant with the first of their two children. Charles dismissed her with some money a little while later, but it didn't last long and she died in Paris, in poverty, in 1658, two years before the Commonwealth collapsed and Charles was invited to return to England to re-establish the old monarchy.

Rumours circulated that Lucy Walter and the prince had in fact

4

married in the town of Liège in 1648, and these rumours were to resurface with ever-increasing regularity through the 1660s and '70s, especially as it became clear that Charles' queen would neither bear the country an heir nor die conveniently and allow him to remarry.

When Charles signed the secret treaty of Dover, he managed to insert a get-out clause for himself: that he would convert to Rome only 'when the interest of the kingdom allowed'. This he managed to spin out until he found himself on his death-bed in February 1685; but, as he died without recognising his popular son as heir, the crown passed smoothly to his

QUEEN ♠

FEAR NOTHING BUT GOD

The late D of M.ˢ Standard.

deeply unpopular younger brother, the Duke of York, who was duly crowned James II. And thus Charles' secret bargain with France was fulfilled; for James was already a Catholic.

James II and the Duke of Monmouth both shared Charles' aristocratic good looks, though neither had a large share of his intelligence. In fact it was not just James II's religion that made him unpopular, although for many English people that would have been enough; he was also arrogant, overbearing, careless and cruel. For a joke like John Wilmot's mock epitaph for Charles II, James might well have had the poet executed. Imagine a Catholic king so widely hated that when, after only three years of his rule, a group of peers invites the king's Protestant daughter and son-in-law over from Holland to take his throne, the move receives a blessing from the Pope. It is perhaps also true that for the Pope, even a Protestant England was better than a Catholic England allied to and dependant upon France.

But this is jumping ahead. Back to 1685.

Where there's Cloth there's Levellers

By contrast to the new King James II of England, the Duke of Monmouth, in exile in Holland, had a reputation for being brave, honest, charming and loyal. And, above all, he was a Protestant.

History is seamless; things do not happen in neat chapters but in an endless stream or web. But to write history is to impose the attitudes of another age upon a single thread of that history pulled out of context: a life, a battle, an affair. And so history must constantly be re-written as we ask new and different questions. The story of Monmouth's rebellion is well known, at least in outline: persuaded that feeling in England was strong enough for himself and against the new King James II, the duke set sail in three ships from Holland to seize the English throne, landing at Lyme in Dorset on 11 June 1685. Three ships carrying 86 men is clearly rather small for an invading army, but it demonstrates the confidence Monmouth felt in raising an army from the ordinary people of the West Country.

But why the West Country? Of course Monmouth could not have sailed straight up the Thames into London with so small a force. Although the people of the capital were strongly opposed to the king, and anti-Catholic, James had become the first British monarch to maintain a regular standing army, and he kept a large part of this army encamped on Blackheath to overawe the populace. By sailing into London, Monmouth would have run straight into these troops. Nor did he have the funds to raise a private army of his own in Holland, as William and Mary would three years later. Monmouth needed a certain amount of time and space to gather his forces and, in the 17th century, the West Country was at least a week from London. Once he had gathered his army, however, he needed to be able to march on London as soon as possible, trusting that public feeling would swell his ranks as he went. Norfolk, Kent and Sussex

The late D. of M & other Rebells taking Shipping for England

were all either too close to London or had strong Royalist connections. Cheshire and the West Country were Monmouth's two favoured routes. Many people from the both areas had fought on Parliament's side against Charles I in the Civil War of the 1640s, and dissenting chapels abounded.

The Late D of M entring Lime with 1500 Men

According to Monmouth's intelligence reports, in the West Country there were fewer noblemen who would side with him than in Cheshire, but probably more commoners. Bristol was also important; it was a major centre of dissent, both political and religious. This distinction is a modern one; no one would have recognised it at the time, and it deserves some explanation. Marxist and other left-wing historians, albeit with notable exceptions, have often missed the religious basis of political dissent in these times, just as much as traditional historians have tried to play down the political implications of religious dissent. We can describe the religious spectrum of 17th century England in political terms, from Right to Left: the Church of England occupies a broad swathe across the centre and to the right, with the authoritarian bishops at the extreme right wing; the Dissenters (Baptists, Independents and others) stretch out to the left, with the Quakers (a little less pacifist than their modern descendants) and Unitarians the most left-wing of those visible.

The Catholics do not fit neatly into this diagram, but James II's authoritarian, hierarchical vision put them, for the moment at least, out on the right wing. It is true that ordinary Catholics had suffered as much as the Dissenters over the preceding years and that they, just like Dissenters, were barred from public office, professions and so on, but James II had started, quite illegally, to pack Catholics into municipal and military positions, causing widespread fear and resentment (even, occasionally, from unwilling Catholics themselves). Still, the ordinary Englishman had neither seen nor met a poor Catholic; Catholics seemed a mysterious cabal of the rich and powerful, much the way

Freemasons and Opus Dei have been viewed in more recent times. What is more, they seemed to be a cabal allied to England's powerful enemies. And furthermore, James II had started to draft Irish Catholic troops into his standing army, already much resented by the people.

Monmouth chose to land in the South-West of England. One of his officers, Nathaniel Wade, wrote:

> A place was therefore thought of to land in the West, the furthest that might be from any standing force, and as near as could be to Taunton, and Resolutions were taken to trust to the People, who by all accounts were well disposed for the design.

Lyme was the port thought best to fit the bill. Monmouth had made a tour of the West Country five years before all this took place, a quasi-'Royal Progress' in which he was well, even rapturously, received throughout the region. His gamble was that the same people who had applauded him then would rally now to the Protestant cause, and indeed many thousands did within days of his landing. Advance news of Monmouth's landing circulated among the Dissenters, and when he landed almost 3000 men were ready to join up immediately.

About a third of these new soldiers were agricultural workers; most of the rest were cloth workers such as weavers and tailors, with plenty of yeomen, shoemakers, and so on. These were in general marginally better off than the farm workers; still poor, but yet with some measure of economic independence. The poorest of farm workers may have remained a little more conservative, or may simply have found it economically impractical to down hoes and join a revolution.

But while the response from the people was excellent, Monmouth faced immediate problems with his commanders. First of all, within a couple of days of the landing, one killed

VIII

Rebells Marching out of Lime

another in an argument over a horse and was promptly dismissed. Next, Monmouth had to send a small force under the command of Lord Grey of Wark, his right-hand man, to deal with the small Royalist garrison at nearby Bridport. At the first sign of conflict Lord Grey turned tail and fled, although his men continued and took the town. Grey's behaviour was disgraceful, but Monmouth decided to keep him on regardless. It may not have been the best decision.

Severall Officers by Command of y̆ King going into y̆ West

The Rebellion

At Lyme, Monmouth published a grand declaration against James II, accusing the king of tyranny and treachery, and of having poisoned his brother Charles II. Monmouth promised freedom of worship for all and that the country should be ruled by parliament (none was sitting at the time; indeed, parliament met only once between 1681 and 1689); and then, with his men, he marched north.

This declaration reached the capital in a couple of days. There it was burnt by the hangman, and a £5000 reward offered for Monmouth's life – a huge sum. But, because the number of men with him was still believed to be small, no regular troops were sent straight away, and the Duke of Albemarle was sent to raise the local militia against him.

The rebels' itinerary ran thus: Taunton, Bristol, Gloucester, London. All were centres of dissent: in 1682, the Mayor of Bridgwater had called Taunton 'this wicked Town . . . the Nursery of rebellion in these Parts' and despaired of the authorities' ability to control its Dissenters. In 1680, the town had prepared and presented to Charles II a petition to exclude James from the throne, and a few years earlier had actually seen troops sent in to collect withheld taxes. What's more, unemployment in the all-important cloth trade in the 1680s surely fomented the spirit of rebellion. Lord Stawell worried in 1683 that this spirit was spreading: 'I wish wee had orders to disarm all the ffanaticks [Dissenters] in ye County', he wrote, and suggested that only more troops could quiet the place.

the godly Maids of Taunton prsenting their Colours upon their knees to ye D. of M.

Ordinary people and ffanaticks flocked to Monmouth's standard as he moved north through Somerset and, by the time he reached Taunton on 18 June, just a week after his landing, he had around 6000 with him, as many people as lived in the town itself. They were shorter of decent arms than of men to bear them.

In Taunton they found 'the Streets so throng'd with People, we could scarce enter . . . their Houses, Doors and Streets garnished with green Boughs, Herbs and Flowers, all the Emblems of Prosperity.'

The Battaile att Bridgwater

Here the duke stayed at 'Captain Hucker's house' opposite the Three Cups Inn (later the County Hotel) and here he made what may have been a terrible mistake. After some demur and debate among his commanders, Monmouth declared himself King of England, 'out of tenderness and for the interest of all our loving subjects, and not upon any motives arising from ourself'. The 'we' is appropriately royal. Confusingly, he would now be James II, and the London King (James II) he would refer to as the Duke of York, his previous title. Helpfully, I shall continue to refer to Monmouth as Monmouth, and only the first James II as James II.

Why should Monmouth's disinterested claiming of the crown have been such a mistake? Historians have generally assumed this to be a natural step: that the rebels were fighting to make Monmouth king. But Monmouth was rallying a very disparate army under his banner, and at the start of the campaign he had stated that he would be no more than the general of the forces he gathered. That there was a debate of any sort at all suggests that some were against this move; that they were not merely Royalists of a different hue. Many, Independents for instance, were of the same ilk as those who back in the 1640s had seen no need for a king at all; they may have thought they had joined a Protestant Republican revolution, and would surely have felt betrayed by this move. Macdonald Wigfield wisely notes: 'That Monmouth aimed at the crown was assumed by all his opponents and half his friends.' Certainly Monmouth gained few new recruits after Taunton, and I see some evidence that this is the point at which some of his men started to desert him.

Nathaniel Wade, a lawyer from Bristol and the son of an officer from Cromwell's New Model Army, states in his account of the rebellion that the suggestion that Monmouth should declare himself king was first made just a few miles south, at Chard, but that it was 'easily ran down by those that were against it'. Then, at Taunton,

> He [Monmouth] took me and some others aside and perswaded us that wee should consent to his being proclaimed King, alledging that according to the intelligence he had received it was a great obstruction to his affaires and the only reason why the Gentlemen of the country came not in to him, being all averse to a Commonwealth, which as he sayd they were all jealous wee intended to sett up . . . Wee submitted to it and it was done.

The bitten lip is palpable. Nevertheless, the republican Wade stuck with his new king. Although Monmouth's reception in Taunton and declaration as king have often been pictured as the highest point in his campaign, they may in another sense have been the beginning of the end, the point at which the movement started to break apart. The Quaker John Whiting, who had been visited by Monmouth five years earlier in Ilchester Gaol, saw him again here and was shocked at how thin and dejected the duke looked.

Two troopes of ye Rebells horse cutt of att Cansham Bridge by Coll: Ogilthorpe

The rebel army moved on, to Bridgwater and Glastonbury, camping in the grounds of the old abbey. Bristol, the second largest city in England, was their next target and, as another hotbed of radical fervour, would almost certainly declare for the rebels. Wade, who knew the city, advised entering from the northeast. The local militias had fought feebly against the rebels in the few skirmishes so far, but another skirmish, this time with the king's cavalry at Keynsham (Cansham Bridge), inflicted some losses on the rebels; and, alarmed at reports that Beaufort had 4000 men stationed in the city, Monmouth made his worst mistake yet. He panicked, and decided to backtrack to gather more forces. The glorious summer weather had broken a few days before, and he marched south in drenching rain, bypassing Royalist Bath, to camp at Radical Frome, his men deserting in droves. Here more bad news came in, of the defeat of a parallel uprising in Scotland under Argyll, and of James II's advance from London with his army. Monmouth saw his momentum gone and his plans beginning to unravel. He was disconsolate, so much so that his officers could barely get orders from him, and he considered the possibility of running away to sea and leaving his men. It was

Ferguson Preaching to the Rebells y' Day before y' Defeat on Iosh. 22. v. 22.

the valiant Lord Grey who dissuaded him, calling the idea 'base'.

Instead, Monmouth retreated to Wells. The London Gazette reports that here his men defaced the Cathedral, 'plundered the Town, and Ravished the Women'; a report probably part truth, part propaganda. It was the king's army who ransacked Frome after the rebels moved on. Monmouth moved next, in desperation, back to Bridgwater, where promised reinforcements failed to materialise, and it was near here, on 6 July, that the Rebellion finally met its disastrous end.

The Battle of Sedgemoor was fought, unusually, in darkness, the proximity of the two armies being discovered by an unplanned pistol shot at about 1 o'clock in the morning, as the duke's troops manoeuvred for a surprise attack. The king's men rallied and routed the rebels; once again it was Grey who gave the order to flee. As a result of this, far more of the rebels were killed in the pursuit than in the battle proper. Of between 3000 and 4000 rebels who took the field, perhaps 300 were killed in the battle and 700 or more in pursuit; 500 rebels taken prisoner on the battlefield were locked in Weston Zoyland church to await trial, another 500 or so were caught in pursuit and 500, or more, by the civil officers afterwards, as rewards were offered for them, and for information on those who had been away from their houses for the past few weeks.

The Late Duke of M: taken
near the Ld Grey

Monmouth himself quit the field about 5 o'clock in the morning; he changed his clothes for a peasant's and headed south-east, aiming for the New Forest, but was caught the next day hiding in a dry ditch covered with ferns. His captors did not at first recognise him with his ragged hair and beard, but were convinced when they found his Garter Star in one overcoat pocket.

In the entire campaign, the king lost about 600 men (two-thirds of those at Sedgemoor), much less than half the rebels' losses. In the aftermath of the battle, 22 captured rebels were strung up on the spot, and a number of the king's men distinguished themselves by their savagery; they were 'still killing them [the rebels] in the corne and hedges and ditches whither they are crept' well after sunrise, and some were later seen pushing wounded men into the graves dug for the dead. The rebellion was effectively over, but the butchery had barely begun; for that, we must introduce the figure of Judge Jeffreys.

'Some Welsh Wolf in Murders nurst . . .'

George Jeffreys was born into a well-to-do family at Acton Park, near Wrexham, in 1645, and went up to London to study Law at the age of 18. The great London Plague two years later created a number of useful openings in the legal profession for an ambitious young man, and he progressed rapidly, gaining a reputation as brutal but efficient.

When the possibility of patronage from the Duchess of Portsmouth came his way, he swiftly ditched an earlier ill-considered connection with the democrats and from thenceforth

Severall Rebells tryed in the West.

he aligned himself whole-heartedly with the 'Court' party. A scurrilous anonymous ballad ('The Duchess of Portsmouth's Picture') from the mid-1670s couples, interestingly, the name of the duchess' protégé with her own antipathy towards the young Duke of Monmouth; it called her

Monmouth's tamer, Jeff's advance
Foe to England, spy of France.

Jeffreys also became a close friend and drinking companion of one Will Chiffinch, a man who the Dictionary of National Biography says 'carried the abuse of backstairs influence to scientific perfection': in short, he was the royal pimp, procuring attractive women for the insatiable Charles II.

In 1678 Jeffreys' first wife died, but he does not seem to have mourned her for long: he remarried and became a father again within just a few months. Another ballad ('A Westminster Wedding, or the Town Mouth') took its title from Jeffreys' appointment as the Recorder of London; a position he described as 'the mouth-piece of the city':

'Tis said when George did dragon slay,
He saved a maid from cruel fray:
But this Sir George, whom knaves do brag on
Mist of the maid, and caught the dragon;
Judge of his merit by his getting:
He's got a ven'mous heart, and tongue
With vipers, snakes and adders hung,
By which, in court, he plays the fury,
Hectors complainant, law, and jury:
His impudence hath all laws broken . . .

His new wife may or may not have been a dragon, but as the widow of the previous Lord Mayor of London, she was yet another useful connection. These latter lines introduce a new thread to Jeffreys' character: he does not appear, for a judge, to have held much scruple over points of law. He would refuse a copy of the indictment to a bailed man or take over the questioning of witnesses if a prosecutor seemed to lack zeal – in other words, he knew himself whether a defendant was guilty or not, and if they were guilty he made sure they were convicted. He was generally thought to be open to appeal upon a single ground only – that the convicted had a powerful friend or ally. In short, he was a servile bully. When a jury back in 1670 had acquitted the Quakers William Penn and William Mead of Riotous Assembly (for praying in the street), Jeffreys' response was to fine the jurors. For, as one might expect, Judge Jeffreys held a dislike, bordering on hatred, for Dissenters; by one account he 'could scarcely be said to command his senses when one of such persuasion was brought before him'. To be fair, he could be equally harsh to Catholics when required, as in the trials following the discovery of the 'Popish Plot' (1678–81), which stirred up popular anti-Catholicism to fever pitch.

Jeffreys worked his way into a

Severall of ȳ Rebells hang'd upon a Tree

succession of useful appoint-
ments; in a few particularly
fruitful months in early 1680
becoming Serjeant, Chief
Justice for the City of Chester,
Solicitor-General to the Duke
of York and then King's
Serjeant. However, he over-
reached himself, and was called
to face a number of charges
from one Lord Delamere;
namely that he had behaved

the Late D: of M: writing
a letter to y^e D of Albemarl

more like a jack-pudding than
with that gravity which beseems
a judge: he was mighty witty
upon the prisoners at the bar,
he was very full of his jokes
upon people that came to give
evidence, not suffering them to
declare what they had to say in
their own way and method, but would interrupt them.

Jeffreys was reprimanded by Parliament for abusing his authority and
had to resign one of his posts (that of Recorder), a move greeted with
joy by the populace: he had few friends among the common people.
But despite occasionally being burnt in effigy by the people of London,
he managed to maintain the favour of the king and his brother, the
Duke of York, and his career was soon back on track. He was created
Baron of Wem in 1681, Chief Justice in 1683, and called to the Privy
Council soon thereafter.

When Charles II died, Jeffreys stood in good favour with the new
King James. But the kind of offices to which he craved admittance
soon began to be filled by Catholics, and though he had principle
enough not to, as many others did at this point, change his religion to
advance his career, he had to think of other ways to advance himself.
And then, as if by providence, the Monmouth Rebellion broke out
down in the South-West of England, was crushed, and George
Jeffreys was sent out with a commission to deal with those of the
rebels still in prison. The eyes of the court and kingdom were upon
him; it was the chance for which he had been waiting the whole of
his life.

The Bloody End

> For had I a thousand Lives, they should be all engaged in support of
> so just a Cause.
>> (Abraham Annesley, on the scaffold, refusing the pardon offered
>> if he would impeach one of his comrades, 30 September 1685)

The captured Duke of Monmouth was taken to the Tower of London.
Compared with the steadfast belief of common rebels like Abraham
Annesley, the duke's own behaviour from the moment of his capture is
not impressive. Ditching the principles in whose name he had led 1500
men to their deaths, he started furiously digging in an attempt to find
himself a way out. He had put a price on the king's head, and led an
army against him, indeed had promised to pursue him as a 'mortal and
bloody Enemy'; it is hard to imagine that he might have hoped to be
pardoned, but he did, and to this end he wrote to the king on 8 July:

> Your Majesty may think it is the misfortune I now lye under makes me
> make this application to you, but I do assure your Majesty it is the re-
> morse I now have in me of the wrong I have done you in several things,
> and now in taking up arms against you . . . my misfortun was such as to
> meet with some horrid people
> that made me believe things of
> your majesty and gave me soe
> many false arguments that I was
> fully lead away to believe that it
> was a shame and a sin before
> God not to doe it. But, Sire, I
> will not trouble your Majesty at
> present with many things I could
> say for myselfe, that I am sure
> would move your compassion the
> chiefest being onely to begg of
> you that I may have that happiness
> as to speak to your Majesty for I
> have that to say to you, Sire, that
> I hope may give you a long and
> happy Reigne. I am sure, Sir,
> when you hear me, you will be
> convinced of the zeale I have for
> your preservation, and how
> heartily I repent of what I have

Rebells plundering the
Loyall Gent: house at Wells

done . . . I shall make an end in begging of your Majesty to believe so well of me that I would rather dy a thousand deaths than to excuse anything I have done, if I did not really think myselfe the most in ye wrong that ever any man was and had not an abhorrence for those that put me upon it, and for the action itself . . . Therefore, Sir, I hope I may live to show you how zealous I shall ever be for your service, and could I say but one word in this letter you would be convinced of it, but it is of that consequence that I dare not do it. Therefore, Sir, I do begg of you once more to let me speak to you, for then you will be convinced how much I shall ever be your Majesties most humble and dutifull

Monmouth

His colours are out; his about turn complete. He was the innocent dupe of wicked rebels, but he is willing to put all that behind him. He blames others: his advisors, his companions; he would blame the people who had fought for him if they weren't beneath his notice. His next letter, four days later, is even worse, for the final card he was offering to play could only be to betray the noblemen in Cheshire who had agreed to side with him. He had no hesitation:

Sir,
I had forgot to tell your Majesty, that it would be very necessary to send some troupes down into Cheshire for there are severall gentlemen there that I believe were ingaged . . . Pray Sir doe not be angry with me if I tell you once more that I long to live to shew you Sir how well and how trully I can serve and if God Almighty sends me that blessing tis all upon earth I will ever aske, being that I hope I shall end my days in showing of you that you have not a truer and faithfuller subject than your most dutifull

Monmouth

Knave

Defnij Executed in Southwarks

The duke did not name the Cheshire noblemen – Lord Delamere, the Earl of

Macclesfield and others – but it seems fairly clear he would do so at the first opportunity. The dowager Queen Catherine then persuaded James II to give his nephew the requested audience, which he did the following day. Some writers have criticised James for granting an interview when he clearly had not the slightest intention of allowing Monmouth to live, but it was not simply sadism that prompted him to let the duke come to beg on his knees; he needed something too. The names of a few disaffected peers were not of enormous consequence to the king, for they would never move against him without a figurehead. What James needed was to discredit the figurehead itself. Giving the craven Monmouth a glimmer of hope for his life, he easily persuaded him to sign a slip of paper that, in the king's eyes, removed all trace of opposition to his rule. It was an affirmation that the duke's mother, Lucy Walter, and Charles II had never been truly married. For, like his brother, James II was a fervent believer in the Divine Right of Kings, and the Tory political theory that had managed to enshrine non-resistance (even to a tyrant) as a tenet of the Church of England. Rebellion against himself was rebellion against God. Only a marriage certificate would have been able, he thought, to unseat him now. The duke signed away his claim to the throne, on his knees, and was carried straight back to the Tower. James now held all the cards.

The late D of M beheaded on Tower Hill 15 july 1685

It is perhaps gruesomely fitting that Monmouth's execution on Tower Hill the following morning was botched, the executioner John Ketch having to make five chops with his axe before he got the head off. This, in the words of Evelyn, 'so incensed the people, that had he not been guarded and got away, they would have torn him to pieces.' Clearly the capital still held more than a little feeling for the Protestant duke and his cause.

Six weeks after Monmouth's execution, Jeffreys' commission set out to try those rebels, well over 1500 in number, still held in the West Country's overflowing gaols. They were to receive about as much mercy as the duke. Even Evelyn, who almost liked Jeffreys, called him 'of nature cruel, and a slave to the Court'. The judge was charged with sending regular reports back to the king upon his progress and it soon became clear that it was not justice but retribution that was his business in the West. The king had been badly frightened by the scale of the rebellion against him.

The commission's first stop was Winchester, on 25 August. There an elderly gentlewoman, Alice Lisle, was charged with sheltering two Dissenters. The two were not rebels (at least they were not named as such), nor had the lady even known what they were doing, but her late husband had been a Cromwellian, and had drawn up Charles I's death warrant in 1649; this was enough to guarantee hers 36 years later. The jury pronounced her not guilty; Jeffreys ordered them to reconsider. Again they returned the same verdict. Fuming, Jeffreys thundered at them that should they do so again he would arrest them all for treason. Pale with fear, the jury returned a third time, this time with a guilty verdict, and the widow was sentenced to be burned at the stake. In response to appeals, Jeffreys lessened the sentence, but only to beheading. There is an interesting note of class here: in executions gentry and aristocrats would always be beheaded, commoners hanged. The result was the same of course, but the process of beheading was seen as more 'dignified' and less degrading. The illegality of the trial is obvious, but the judge in question was the Lord Chief Justice, and most of the West of England was under virtual martial law. He could do as he liked.

At Salisbury, six defendants each received a fine and a flogging, and then in Dorchester on 4 September, the Assizes began in earnest. The judge gave out that if anyone hoped for mercy they should plead guilty at once and not waste the court's time. Twenty-nine did so, and were immediately sentenced to death. The commission then made their bloody way to Taunton, Wells and Bristol, trying hundreds of cases a day. Over 560 were tried in three days at Taunton Castle, and nearly a third of them sentenced to death. The condemned were then sent back out to be hanged in their home towns, which were almost every town and village in Somerset, Dorset and North Devon. Those bullied into pleading guilty were hanged straight away; many others on the slenderest of evidence or hearsay. 'Aiding and abetting' the rebels could stretch to having had your horse stolen by them – the penalty was death. At Lyme, Christian Battiscombe's fiancée pleaded for his life: the judge replied that he could spare only part of him, but she could name that part and have it. John Madders would probably have been pardoned, but that one of the witnesses in his favour overdid it, calling him a good Protestant. 'Oho!' said the judge, 'he is a Presbyterian. I can smell them forty miles. He shall be hanged!'

In all, 331 people were executed; most were hanged, quartered and parts of their bodies were boiled in tar and strung up around the towns. Another 850 were sold as slaves to the king's colonies in Barbados and Jamaica (11 were subsequently pardoned, and others transported in their place) and a further 408 fined, whipped or given prison sentences.

'The country overflowed with blood', wrote Joshua Toulmin, in his *History of Taunton* (1791; revised 1822):

One Pitts is to be W̅h̅i̅p̅t̅ through every Town in Dorsetshire for Seaven Years together

Every part of it shewed spectacles, at which decency blushed, and humanity shuddered. The rites of funeral were denied to those who suffered; the houses and steeples were covered with their heads; and the trees laden almost as thick with quarters, as with leaves. The eye was everywhere shocked with sight of carcases; and the bleeding hearts of the relatives were again wounded with the view of a parent's, a son's or a brother's limbs.

And parents they were, at least as many as sons. An excellent study by Peter Earle of the rebels of 1685 has indicated that the great majority of them were over the age of 25, and perhaps a third over 40. Quite a few were over 60. Furthermore, as there was in most cases only one person of each surname among the rebels, Earle suggests that each family may have nominated one male, often an older man, a father or uncle, to join the rebellion whilst the rest continued to work. In Taunton and Lyme, where a third of all adult males fought under Monmouth's banner, this suggests that almost the entire population must have sided with the rebellion; certainly everyone must have had acquaintances or relatives among the convicted. Another grisly account, quoted in Woolrych, describes

the houses and steeples covered as close with heads, as at other times frequently in that country with crows or ravens. Nothing could be liker hell than all those parts; nothing so like the devil as he [Jeffreys]. Caldrons hizzing, carkases boyling, pitch and tar sparkling and glowing, blood and limbs boyling, and tearing, and mangling, and he the great director of all.

On his way to the West, Jeffreys had said that if he did not depopulate the place, it would not be his fault; on the way back, he boasted that he had hanged more men than all the judges of England since William the Conqueror. Upon his return to London he was paid handsomely for his work – over £1400 – and soon after this, he received his real reward: James created him Lord Chancellor of England.

Some have attributed Jeffreys' severity at these Assizes to pain from a kidney stone. This could never excuse his behaviour, but the real answer is far simpler: it was a cold career move. He is possibly the most despicable figure in British history. Perhaps James II might steal that honour – it's a close call. Jeffreys was the kind of vicious bureaucrat who can only thrive as a servant of tyranny, and there he was in his element. A relentless careerist, as slippery as an eel but without the charm, he had no conscience and no regard either for others' consciences or for their lives. When one of Jeffreys' earliest biographers, Humphrey Woolrych, told a friend what he was planning to write, his friend exclaimed: 'Why, you surely are not going to whitewash *Judge Jeffreys?*' It is a comment that perhaps says as much about the art of biography in the 1820s as it does about anything else, but that aside, the whitewash simply could not be done: he was a man for whom there really are no excuses. Woolrych makes a brief effort at one point to justify Jeffreys' conduct – '[he] was involved with sons of violence, and it was not more than his duty, pledged by oaths, to crush them' – but he cannot refrain from adding to it Dryden's translation of a couplet from Juvenal:

> Great men to great crimes owe their plate embost
> Fair palaces, and furniture of cost.

A Saddle on his Back

VI ♠

The late D. of M. Ld Grey & a German carried to y^e Tower

One of the Scottish rebels, on the scaffold in Edinburgh on 26 June, declared: 'I am sure there was no Man born marked of God above another; for none comes into the world with a Saddle on his Back, neither any Booted and Spurr'd to Ride him.' In contrast to the fate of the poorer rebels, many of their leaders, men like Goodenough, Ffoulkes, and the German, Buys, survived. The Reverend Hook, Monmouth's chaplain, turned Catholic. Nathaniel Wade led a party of men away from the battlefield, seized a small ship at Ilfracombe and attempted to escape the country. They were forced back into shore by two frigates, and there the rebels dispersed. Wade was captured a little while after; he obtained a pardon in exchange for a confession, which it was hoped would implicate others. However, although his narrative is one of our best first-hand sources for what actually happened, he was extremely careful not to name any-one in it who was not already dead, or otherwise safe in exile. Again and again he writes: 'and some others, whose names I cannot remember'. It was a fine performance. James II later developed considerable respect for the man, and after his pardon he even gave Wade the post of Town Clerk of Bristol.

Lord Grey made a confession too, but his was far less careful than Wade's; like the Duke of Monmouth, Grey's primary concern was to deflect blame from himself. He also had a powerful ally; the Earl of Rochester was making a fortune from Grey's sequestered estates, which would revert to Grey's brother upon his death, and so pulled out all the stops to keep Grey alive.

Small bands of rebels were hidden by friends and sympathisers in the West Country for months; some escaped to Holland, and others lay low, foraging on the edge of towns until the king issued his general pardon for rebels (with a number of exceptions) in March 1686. A plan of some of the exiled rebels to set up a manufacture of 'English Cloth'

25

in Holland was seen as a serious threat to the country's trade, and they were offered pardons if they returned with their goods. Many of the rebels had melted away from Monmouth's army well before Sedgemoor, and not all of these were subsequently caught. What's more, given the questionable methods of the Assize trials, it is clear that many were executed or transported who had only peripheral sympathies, if even those, with the rebellion. Nevertheless it is also quite clear that it really was the common people who bore the brunt of the retribution, and that the harsh measures of the Bloody Assizes worked: both the rebellion and the spirit of rebellion in the region were crushed.

James II's high-handed and contemptuous attitude to his subjects was not, however, to last much longer. Despite making attempts over the next couple of years to win the Dissenters back over to his side as allies against the Church of England, the country lurched from crisis to crisis. The final straw was the surprise birth of a son and heir to the throne: a Catholic heir. Although the birth was widely believed to be an imposture (the boy's son would return to Britain a few decades later as 'Bonnie Prince Charlie'), James' reign collapsed and his protestant daughter Mary was invited with her husband William of Orange to come over from Holland and take his throne. They too landed in South Devon to march on London, on 5 November (the traditional anti-Catholic day) 1688, but James fled the country with hardly a fight, dropping the Great Seal into the Thames as he went.

These moves were greeted warmly in the West Country, of course, but it is still plain to see that this, the 'Glorious Revolution', was a far cry from the popular republican revolution for which so many had fought and died at Sedgemoor. It was instead a pragmatic settlement that did little to alter the social order; a compromise between Whig and Tory, not to overthrow the law but to confirm it against a law-breaking king, and a triumph more for parliament than for anyone else. The Revolution Settlement of 1689 set the shape of the modern British political system. For this it is much applauded. In Ireland, always seen as a gateway for French (i.e. Catholic) invasion, it was a bitter re-conquest that, likewise, set the shape of troubles still unresolved today.

At least six of Monmouth's officers, and an unspecified number of men, returned to England among William of Orange's army. Some of those transported to America also made it back to Britain over the next few years. The 'poor country cloth-workers' of 1685 became Protestant martyrs, and history swiftly swept all their various causes together into one. Traces of the more radical elements were wiped where possible, but some can still be found between the lines. A collection of the rebels' dying speeches was soon published; it went through several editions, becoming the *Western Martyrology*. It may seem to a modern reader unremittingly pious, but nevertheless, in the long dedicatory poem we find the lines:

> If ill Designs some to the Battle drew,
> 'Tis impious to condemn all for a few.

Further on in the book, we even learn of the presence of some atheists, who,

> because God does not think fit to govern the World according to their Minds, impudently announce, That there is no God at all, That Religion's a meer Cheat, and Heaven and Hell but Priest-craft and Fable.

Strong stuff for the 1680s.

Lord Grey, the only aristocrat other than Monmouth actually involved in the rebellion, had his title restored to him by James II, then pretended a riding accident to excuse him from going to James' defence when William of Orange landed. He later became a loyal subject of the new King William and was rewarded with the titles of Viscount and Earl of Tankerville, before dying in 1701.

And what of our friend George Jeffreys? As William of Orange landed, this man whom John Carter in the *Western Martyrology* was to brand 'the darling Brat of Hell' decided that his time in the country was up. He changed his clothes for those of a poor seaman and fled to the nearest port, hoping to take a passage on a collier to Hamburg. However, he was recognised in an inn at Wapping (quite probably by someone who had been up in court before him) and seized by a mob. The Train-bands (police) rescued him from them, but in the Tower of London he fell ill, and there he died just a few months later, before he could be brought to trial for his atrocities.

There have been too many books on this subject – particularly biographies of Monmouth – for me to wish to list them all; many contain good bibliographies. *The Western Martyrology* (4th edition, 1693; 5th edition, 1705), Richard Locke's *The Western Rebellion* (1782) and L.E.J. Brooke's unpublished 'Notes on Taunton' are, however, all valuable sources. Of the more recent histories, Peter Earle's *Monmouth's Rebels* (1977) and W.M. Wigfield's *The Monmouth Rebellion: a Social History* (1980) seem to deserve especial praise; Robert Dunning's *The Monmouth Rebellion* (1984) is a fine overall survey.

I would like to thank Dani, Michael, and the staff of the Somerset Studies Library at Taunton for their help.